EAB922-Women in Science (eBook)

ABDO Publishing Company 6 Volumes Flipbook
Set Price: $251.70
Reading Level: 8th Grade
Interest Level: Middle
Accelerated Reader: No

Women play an essential role in science and have made a lasting impact on how we understand our world. Women in Science provides junior high and high school readers with biographical information on some of the greatest women in science, as well their discoveries and contributions to their respective fields of science and the world. Aligned to Common Core Standards and correlated to state standards. Essential Library is an imprint of Abdo Publishing, a division of ABDO.

Title	Code	List Price	Our Price	Copyright	Prg
Chien-Shiung Wu: Nuclear Physicist	EAB788310	$59.93	$41.95	2018	
Grace Hopper: Computer Scientist	EAB788297	$59.93	$41.95	2018	
Jane Goodall: Primatologist and Conservationist	EAB788280	$59.93	$41.95	2018	
Mae Carol Jemison: Astronaut and Educator	EAB788303	$59.93	$41.95	2018	
Marie Curie: Chemist and Physicist	EAB788266	$59.93	$41.95	2018	
Rosalind Franklin: DNA Discoverer	EAB788273	$59.93	$41.95	2018	

D1088315

WOMEN
IN SCIENCE

JANE GOODALL

PRIMATOLOGIST AND CONSERVATIONIST

By Michael Capek

Content Consultant
Randall Susman, PhD
Professor and Chair, Department of Anatomical Sciences
Stony Brook University

Essential Library

An Imprint of Abdo Publishing | abdopublishing.com

ABDOPUBLISHING.COM

Published by Abdo Publishing, a division of ABDO, PO Box 398166, Minneapolis, Minnesota 55439. Copyright © 2018 by Abdo Consulting Group, Inc. International copyrights reserved in all countries. No part of this book may be reproduced in any form without written permission from the publisher. Essential Library™ is a trademark and logo of Abdo Publishing.

Printed in the United States of America, North Mankato, Minnesota
042017
092017

Cover Photo: Kathy Willens/AP Images
Interior Photos: CSU Archives/Everett Collection Inc/Alamy, 4, 45; M. H. Gallery/iStockphoto, 8, 41; Jeryl Tan/iStockphoto, 12; Shutterstock Images, 14, 29; The Jane Goodall Institute, 16, 21; Apic/Hulton Archive/Getty Images, 24; AP Images, 30, 67; Mark Chentx/iStockphoto, 31; Ferenc Szelepcsenyi/Shutterstock Images, 34; CBS Photo Archive/CBS/Getty Images, 36, 48, 62; Paul Stringer/Shutterstock Images, 39 (background); Globe Turner/Shutterstock Images, 39 (foreground); Stephen Robinson/NHPA/Photoshot/Newscom, 46; Bettmann/Getty Images, 52, 84; Guenter Guni/iStockphoto, 58; Dorling Kindersley/Getty Images, 61 (top), 61 (middle right), 61 (middle left), 61 (bottom); Sepp Friedhuber/iStockphoto, 65; MJ Photography/Alamy, 69; UA_IFTN_NEU/United Archives GmbH/Alamy, 72; iStockphoto, 75, 76; Michael Nichols/National Geographic, 79; Mayela Lopez/AFP/Getty Images, 82; Hendrik Schmidt/AFP/Getty Images, 88–89; Enrique Cuneo/GDA/AP Images, 91; Duffy-Marie Arnoult/WireImage/Getty Images, 94; Krista Kennell/Shutterstock Images, 97

Editor: Valerie Bodden
Series Designer: Nikki Farinella

PUBLISHER'S CATALOGING–IN–PUBLICATION DATA

Names: Capek, Michael, author.
Title: Jane Goodall: primatologist and conservationist / by Michael Capek.
Other titles: Primatologist and conservationist
Description: Minneapolis, MN : Abdo Publishing, 2018. | Series: Women in
    science | Includes bibliographical references and index.
Identifiers: LCCN 2016962325 | ISBN 9781532110436 (lib. bdg.) |
    ISBN 9781680788280 (ebook)
Subjects: LCSH: Goodall, Jane, 1934- --Juvenile literature. | Primatologists--
    England--Biography--Juvenile literature. | Women primatologists--England--
    Biography--Juvenile literature. | Chimpanzees--Tanzania--Gombe Stream
    National Park--Juvenile literature.
Classification: DDC 590.92 [B]--dc23
LC record available at http://lccn.loc.gov/2016962325

CONTENTS

CLOSE ENCOUNTERS

Jane Goodall had been roaming the steep hills and thorny thickets of Gombe Stream Nature Preserve since first light one morning in August 1960. Like most other days since she had arrived in Tanzania one month previously, she had not seen any of the elusive creatures she'd come to study. The country's dense forests and valleys, she had discovered, might be the ideal places for a chimpanzee, but they were not the most pleasant environment for a human who wished to observe the animals up close.

Many days, she heard chimps, and she occasionally spied them far off through binoculars. Usually, though, they were long gone by the time she reached the place where she first spotted them. Reports from locals said more than 150 chimps lived in

Jane Goodall was 26 years old when she began her research at Gombe Stream Nature Preserve.

Gombe Stream

Gombe Stream became a national park in 1968. Located approximately 10 miles (16 km) north of the town of Kigoma, Tanzania, the park encompasses only 20 square miles (52 sq km), making it the smallest of Tanzania's national parks. Dense jungle covers much of the area, and the terrain is rugged and hilly.

The park sits along the northern end of Lake Tanganyika. Approximately 410 miles (660 km) long and from 10 to 45 miles (16 to 72 km) wide, this lake is essentially a long, narrow, inland sea, holding some of the purest and clearest water in Africa. It is also the second-deepest lake in the world, with a depth of 4,710 feet (1,436 m).

the Gombe preserve, but Goodall had not seen more than a few dozen.[1] Although she was frustrated, Goodall knew the chimps had good reason to keep their distance. Relations between chimps and local villagers had never been particularly peaceful. Hunters illegally caught chimps for food or the pet trade or killed them as pests for raiding crops, gardens, and sometimes homes.

Over the next few months, Goodall learned that getting close enough to observe the daily habits of the secretive and wary creatures was more than frustrating and bewildering. It was often downright dangerous. Gombe's treacherous terrain was full of cliffs and jagged rocks hidden by lush foliage. The thick grasslands and jungles provided ample cover for baboons, leopards, and some of the world's most venomous snakes. Insects were a particular problem, especially Africa's notorious tsetse flies and disease-carrying mosquitos. Two military-surplus tents provided only little protection. Within three months of their arrival, Goodall and her mother, Vanne, who had come to help her get settled, were stricken with malaria. Both spent more than a week with raging fevers, barely able to leave their cots.

Despite the difficulties, Goodall was not the kind of person to give up easily on a dream, particularly one she'd had since she was eight years old. As soon as her fever subsided, though still weak from her illness, she resumed her daily search for the chimps.

FIRST ENCOUNTERS

That steamy August day had been business as usual. She had seen a few chimps and pursued them slowly and carefully, not attempting to hide or keep particularly quiet. Her experience with animals told her sneaking up on them was not the best way to establish trust. The chimps knew she was there. She decided to wait for them to come to her with the same sense of curiosity and wonder she felt for them.

Goodall found a strategic point to survey the valley and sat that afternoon on a high point she named the Peak. This became her favorite place because of the wide, panoramic view it provided of the surrounding hills, cliffs, and valleys and of the glistening Lake Tanganyika. Occasionally, when she was lucky, Goodall's strategic high perch allowed glimpses of chimps

From her perch in Gombe Stream, Goodall had a view of Lake Tanganyika.

feeding in trees or passing in groups below. Early in her study, the wary chimpanzees kept their distance.

But that day, as Goodall later reported, her "heart missed several beats" when a small group of chimps appeared on a hilltop very suddenly and very close.[2] She recognized one of them from an earlier encounter. He was a large male with a lustrous black coat and a distinctive silvery beard. The other two chimps hurried past her, but the bearded male stopped approximately ten paces away, turned, and looked at her. With what Goodall described as an expression of intense curiosity, turning his head from side to side, the chimp studied her for several minutes before scampering off to join the others.

Several days later, Goodall encountered the same male in the forest. He passed within a few yards of the conspicuous spot where she had chosen to sit, along a well-worn path. This time, the chimp did not pause or look at her, but she was beginning to feel she might be on the verge of making a real connection. The chimp appeared to be comfortable presenting himself to her.

Encouraged, Goodall increased her efforts to approach the chimps. Every day, she would rise at dawn and dress in drab-colored clothes. Then, always staying in view, she would move to where she anticipated the chimps would be. If she heard chimps approaching, she would sit and pretend she was not interested in them so they would not perceive her as a threat. Also to minimize the chance of threatening the chimps, she picked leaves, pretended to chew them, self-groomed, and pawed at the ground, imitating gestures and sounds she had observed in the chimps.

Goodall took detailed notes about the behaviors she observed and the foods the chimps ate. She noted and attempted to imitate the many different sounds she heard coming from the chimps. She tried to understand different vocalizations and to associate and match certain behaviors to

Chimp Salad

Wild chimps spend almost half of every day eating, and Gombe provides a wide variety of food for them to eat. Goodall found that chimps dine on termites and other insects, as well as palm nuts, fruit, eggs, berries, and meat (mainly monkeys, bush pig, bushbuck, and other small mammals). They also eat large quantities of vegetation, often alternating bites of leaves with whatever else they're eating.

specific sounds. She was able to identify grunts of pleasure while they were feeding or grooming and what she called "pant-hoots" of excitement or warning.[3] In the early stages of her research, making sense of chimp vocalizations was still very difficult.

REDEFINING HUMAN

Weeks passed, and Goodall noticed the silver-bearded male ambling or romping nearby with increasing frequency during her daily rambles. It happened far too often to be mere accident. Occasionally, the chimp would look at her, but mostly he only altered his path to pass within a few paces of her before he disappeared into the tall grass and forest vegetation. Goodall began to notice other chimps examining her as well, watching from high tree branches or peeping from behind leafy bushes. Only the gray-bearded chimp regularly approached close enough for her to see and describe his individual features and gestures.

Then, in October, almost at the end of her allotted time at Gombe, Goodall witnessed a startling scene. Early one morning, she heard loud screams and breaking branches in a tree nearby. She moved closer and saw three chimps eating, sharing what she described as "something that looked pink."[4] She could not see what the chimps were eating, but from the noisy and panicked behavior of bush pigs under the tree, she concluded that the chimps had caught and killed a piglet. Goodall's observation confirmed what scientists had theorized: chimpanzees were carnivorous and predatory. She was the first to record that wild chimps not only eat meat but also share it willingly. This social behavior had never been observed or recorded in any primate other than humans.

A week later, Goodall made another, even more startling discovery. That morning, she once again happened upon the silver-chinned chimp, whom she called David Graybeard in her notes. He was sitting atop a termite mound, engrossed in an activity. David saw

Coordinated Hunting

Early on, Goodall believed chimps' capture of prey was individual and accidental, a result of finding a bush pig or baboon babies on the ground, for instance. Eventually, however, she observed that when hunting certain prey, such as monkeys, chimps actually work together in a highly coordinated effort to capture and then eat and often share the meat. She described one monkey hunt this way:

> Before starting to hunt in earnest, the chimpanzees often spend time on the ground gazing up into the canopy, or walking below as the monkeys leap above them. It seems they are assessing the situation: the availability of suitable victims, particularly mother-infant pairs and small juveniles; where they are located; and probably the arboreal [tree] pathways along which the monkeys would be able to escape.[5]

Goodall but didn't run away, even as several other chimps with him fled. While Goodall watched, David carefully and purposefully poked a long stem of dried grass into a hole in the termite mound. When he pulled the grass up a moment later, the stem was coated with clinging termites, which Goodall later learned are among chimps' favorite foods. David nibbled off the insects and reinserted the grass probe. For nearly an hour, she watched him fishing for termites. Later, when his grass stem broke, he selected another, stouter twig, stripped it of leaves,

Chimps may spend up to four hours a day fishing for termites, which provide needed minerals, fat, and protein.

Crafty Chimps

Goodall's research at Gombe revealed that chimpanzees make and use a variety of tools in their daily lives. Aside from termite fishing, chimps fashion and use sticks and stems as probes to dip honey from beehives and as clubs to knock down fruit and nuts from trees. They also use rocks as hammers to open tough nuts, and wads of leaves act as sponges to clean their bodies and to get water or sap to drink from deep holes in trees. Goodall noted that chimps frequently find and reuse the same tools, some of them for many months. She also observed chimps using objects just for fun, which she insisted in her records was just another form of tool use. Chimps use rocks and round fruit for ball games and palm fronds and sticks for tug-of-war matches. They often use sticks and other objects to scratch and tickle themselves, too. Self-tickling, Goodall noted, is a favorite game, particularly for young chimps, who often rub or poke ticklish areas of their bodies with sticks or stones while rolling on the ground, making a sound that she said "somewhat resembles human laughter."[6]

and chewed it into a better tool. He proceeded to use it with great skill to collect termites.

The implications of what Goodall had witnessed were enormous. Chimpanzee meat-eating was an exciting discovery, but the discoveries of toolmaking and tool modifying were revolutionary. In the mid-1900s, scientists believed the terms *toolmaker* and *tool-user* were part of the definition of being human. To distinguish human ancestors from species that were not human ancestors, archaeologists and anthropologists looked at whether the species had crafted and used tools.

When Goodall wrote to tell her friend and mentor Louis Leakey what she had found, he was stunned. Leakey was one of the world's leading scientists and had spent his life searching for the remains of humankind's oldest ancestors. Leakey sent back a telegram that summed up the significance of her discovery: "Now we must redefine 'tool,' redefine 'man,' or accept chimpanzees as human."[7]

As writer Carol Lee Flinders said, "Goodall's discoveries that first year were groundbreaking: If she had done nothing else for the rest of her life, her place in the history of science would have been secure."[8]

But Goodall's primate research was only beginning. Other discoveries that would further expand knowledge and perceptions about chimpanzees and humankind were still to come. Goodall's work would eventually change the practice of field science and make her what one writer described as "the most widely celebrated woman scientist of our century."[9]

Goodall's early work at Gombe led to a lifetime of studying and protecting chimps.

CHAPTER
TWO

WILD BEGINNINGS

Jane Goodall's fascination with animals began almost from the time she was born on April 3, 1934, in London, England. For her first birthday, Jane's father, Mortimer, gave her Jubilee, a fuzzy toy replica of a real baby chimpanzee born at the London Zoo only two months earlier. Jubilee immediately became Jane's favorite plaything and remained one of her most cherished possessions throughout her life.

Jane soon discovered that live creatures were even more fascinating than her toy. She grew up in Bournemouth, England, a seaside resort town on the English Channel, 94 miles (151 km) southwest of London. Her family home, called the Birches, was an old Victorian house located near a small hotel and family farms. All around were trees and hills to climb and fields and

Jane's love of animals began early, with her stuffed toy chimpanzee Jubilee, and never faded.

woods to roam. Jane loved spending time with family and friends but was always happiest alone in nature, wandering brushy paths, climbing trees, and chasing rabbits, foxes, and hedgehogs. She brought home whatever interested her, from shells and snails to bugs and worms. Jane's mother, Vanne, never scolded her about getting dirty or bringing home smelly creatures. "I was never, ever told I couldn't do something because I was a girl," she later remembered.[1]

FAMILY SUPPORT

Growing up, Jane had little contact with men or boys. Her father and other male relatives were rarely home, and Jane's parents divorced when she was 12 years old. Young Jane was surrounded by a group of strong, patient, and supportive

War Lessons

Jane was 11 years old when World War II (1939–1945) ended. Although she suffered no real physical or mental injuries, the war affected her deeply. German bombs sometimes exploded near her home, and she and her family spent many terrifying nights in air raid shelters. Her uncle died in the war, and her father did not return either, choosing to live apart from the family. Yet, the real difficulty for Jane came when the war in Europe ended. In its wake, news stories appeared revealing the almost unthinkable scale of human suffering. Particularly disturbing were photos of German concentration camps where millions of innocent people had died. The grim reality of the Holocaust shattered Jane's belief in the basic decency of humans. She later said she was never able to erase the images or the horror from her memory.

women: grandmothers, aunts, and cousins. Jane remembered her childhood with fondness and her mostly female family members as funny, smart, bright, brave, and fiercely supportive of one another, particularly her. Later, she saw a close similarity between her own upbringing and chimpanzee child-rearing, in which nurturing females, particularly mothers, play the key role.

Jane's family recognized her gifts when she was very young. They especially noted her powers of imagination and mental focus. As her biographer, Dale Peterson, observed, "From an early age she seems to have possessed a capacity for focused attention and a mental clarity that was readily transported from inner to outer, from dreaming to waking, from vision to action."[2] In other words, Jane could harness her natural enthusiasm and focus on whatever goal she had in mind. Throughout her life, that goal often involved animals. Jane became a patient, curious observer of nature.

One summer day, when she was five years old, Jane disappeared. Her parents, grandparents, aunts and uncles, and the police searched frantically for hours but couldn't find a trace of her. Finally, just before dark, someone spotted the dirty, tired, and hungry little girl walking toward home. When her mother asked her gently where she'd been for the past five hours, Jane answered simply, "With a hen."[3] She had sat all afternoon, oblivious to the stifling heat and clamor outside, watching hens

A Father's Influence

Growing up, Jane rarely saw her father, Mortimer, who traveled widely as an engineer, race car driver, and military officer. But he still influenced his daughter's life. According to Jane's biographer, Dale Peterson, inheriting the genes of a smart, adventurous, and tough-minded father helped Jane grow into "a woman with a race car driver's constitution; good eyesight, high energy, a natural and happy competitiveness, a capacity for intense and extended concentration, a surprising attraction to risk, and an unusual tolerance for physical stress and [motion sickness]."[4]

lay eggs in a neighbor's chicken coop.

Despite the worry she had caused, neither Jane's mother nor anyone in her family made Jane feel she had done anything wrong. Jane was just being Jane. She was taken home, fed, and bathed, and her family listened intently as she explained what she had learned from her experience.

THE ALLIGATOR CLUB

For young Jane, any experience without an animal involved was not an experience worth having. For her, animals were never only pets. They were companions and friends, thinking and feeling beings with whom to share good times and have adventures. She could hardly imagine a life without animals, and from the age of eight, when anyone asked about her future, she said that one day she would go to Africa and live with wild animals. At the time, she was not thinking specifically of studying chimps. Instead, she pictured Africa as the perfect place to encounter the largest possible variety of fascinating creatures.

Although Jane would become famous for her work with chimps, dogs were always her favorite animals.

You Tarzan. Me Jane.

Edgar Rice Burroughs's *Tarzan* series of books strongly influenced young Jane. "It was daydreaming about life in the forest with Tarzan that led to my determination to go to Africa, to live with animals and write books about them," she later said. "I was madly in love with the Lord of the Jungle."[6] But she was not at all impressed with the fictional Jane, whom she believed was much too weak and whiny. "She was a *wimp*. . . . I always knew I'd have been a far better mate for him," she said.[7]

In the meantime, as she grew up, Jane kept a collection of animals around the house, in her room, and in the yard. She took responsibility for feeding, cleaning up after, and playing with her collection of pampered creatures. At one time, her collection included snails, legless lizards, a tortoise, a guinea pig, a cat, hamsters, and a canary. She also took care of and played with a wide assortment of dogs, including her own and any in the neighborhood she thought looked hungry or lonesome.

Even though she spent much time caring for animals, Jane felt helpless when one day she came upon a group of boys catching and pulling the legs off of crabs at the seashore. She yelled at the boys, but they only laughed. That day, feeling outnumbered and defeated, Jane simply turned away. Forty years later, she wrote, "I am still ashamed of myself. Why didn't I try harder to stop them from tormenting those crabs?"[5]

Later, when she was 12 years old, Jane organized a group she named the Alligator Club, through which she encouraged a deep study and appreciation of nature and animals. Jane wrote, illustrated, and mailed out a newsletter and organized nature hikes and excursions for collecting shells, insects, and feathers. In 1951, the club set a goal of raising money to assist local efforts to rescue old horses from slaughter. From that time on, Jane's passion for animal welfare would continue to grow.

Rusty

"I had a marvelous teacher in animal behavior throughout my childhood—my dog Rusty," Jane once wrote.[8] Rusty was a black and white spaniel that for much of Jane's childhood followed her everywhere she went. With Rusty by her side, Jane later wrote:

> I learned to crawl through dense undergrowth, scramble up sheer slopes, and creep silently along narrow trails. In sunshine and rain, heat and cold, those [places] were my training ground where I developed the skills that were to stand me in such good stead in the forests of Gombe.[9]

CHAPTER
THREE

AFRICA IN MY BLOOD

G oodall performed exceptionally well in high school and graduated near the top of her class at age 18. Unlike many of her friends, she did not go immediately to college. She could not afford to pay tuition and refused to allow her family to pay her way. Goodall's only career goal was the same one she'd had since age eight. She wanted to live in Africa and work with animals. No other options seemed to make any sense.

Outwardly, Goodall never wavered, but privately, she was worried that her African dreams were far-fetched and unrealistic. Her family remained uncritical and supportive. Goodall later wrote, "My mother always used to say, 'Jane, if you really want something, and you really work hard and you take advantage of opportunities, and above all if you never

Goodall never gave up on her childhood dream of living in Africa.

give up, you will find a way.'"[1] Acting on her mother's advice, Goodall took secretarial and business courses. Her mother reasoned that these courses would provide her with typing and organizational skills that would be valuable no matter what direction her life took.

For two years, Goodall worked at office jobs. She had an active social life and even seriously considered accepting an offer of marriage from a man she was dating. But she realized a quiet home life was not part of her dream. She ended the relationship and kept working at office jobs, hoping something more exciting was just around the corner.

Theosophy

In 1955, Goodall enrolled in a philosophy class at the London School of Economics. The class was based on principles of theosophy, a spiritually focused approach to living based largely on Buddhist-inspired concepts such as meditation. The class helped Goodall hone inborn skills she knew she already possessed. She was well aware of her ability to move inward, to control her mind and body to block out physical discomfort and even pain, and to focus her thoughts with laser sharpness. These would become powerful tools she would use in her work at Gombe.

AFRICA

In the summer of 1955, an exciting opportunity presented itself. Clo Mange, a friend from high school, wrote to ask Goodall if she would like to come to Kenya, which was under British control at that time. Mange and her family had moved there, and she remembered Goodall's often-repeated wish to visit Africa.

Goodall decided to take a chance. She quit her job and began preparations to visit her friend in Africa. She would stay for six months, she decided, and see what developed. If nothing did, she would return to England and find a better job—or marry, perhaps. She was smart and attractive. She already had another offer from an enthusiastic suitor who was willing to wait.

On March 13, 1957, Goodall boarded a passenger ship bound for Africa. A month later, she wrote home: "I really do simply adore Kenya. It is so wild, uncultivated, primitive, mad, exciting, unpredictable. . . . On the whole I am living in the Africa I have always longed for, always felt stirring in my blood."[2]

OLDUVAI GORGE

In mid-May 1957, a friend casually mentioned Louis Leakey to Goodall. Leakey and his wife Mary were the world's leading paleoanthropologists, and they lived and worked nearby in Nairobi. "If you are interested in animals," the friend said, "you must meet Louis Leakey."[3] Goodall did not wait for a formal introduction. She phoned Leakey immediately and arranged a visit.

Leakey and Goodall met at the Corydon Museum in Nairobi (now the Nairobi National Museum), where Leakey was head curator. As Leakey showed Goodall around, he bombarded her with questions to test her knowledge about various exhibits they viewed. The famed scientist appeared to be impressed by Goodall's natural intelligence and knowledge of animals. He especially liked the fact that she had office skills. At the end of the tour, Leakey asked if she would like to work as his secretary at the museum. Perhaps, he suggested, she might also assist him and Mary at their excavations in Tanzania's Olduvai Gorge.

Goodall spent the summer working with the Leakeys at Olduvai. She organized and typed lists of artifacts and fossils and prepared reports and letters describing the fossils and stone tools. The Leakeys also gave Goodall the opportunity to get into the excavations and dig. She made a few small finds, including fossilized teeth and bones. The experience affected her tremendously. Her record-keeping tasks taught her scientific language and modes of presentation. More than this, the experience introduced her to the hard work of science and ignited in her a thirst for further discovery.

Olduvai Gorge

Olduvai Gorge is a natural and archaeological treasure, located near Serengeti National Park in northern Tanzania. Made up of two steep, intersecting ravines, the gorge is approximately 300 feet (90 m) deep and 30 miles (50 km) long. Its jagged gashes were carved over time by rivers and a series of violent geological events. For paleoanthropologists such as Louis and Mary Leakey, the natural exposures cut into the earth's crust were like an open window into the distant past, allowing access to layers of fossil-bearing rocks that included primate stone tools millions of years old.

Olduvai Gorge is one of the most important paleoanthropological sites in the world.

Most of all, Olduvai was a fulfillment of hopes she'd had since she was a child. This was the Africa of her dreams: living with wild animals, sleeping under the stars, and working in the blazing heat. As she wrote to her mother, "I am doing the things I have always dreamed of doing. . . . I do, very often, wonder if I am dreaming—& if not what I have done to deserve such luck."[4]

In the evenings and during breaks from work, she loved to listen to Louis Leakey's stories. Goodall soaked up every word. One of Leakey's favorite topics was a group of chimpanzees that lived on the shores of Lake Tanganyika several hundred miles to the west. The area, called Gombe, was isolated from human contact, except for a few villages. Its lushly forested, rugged terrain provided ideal chimpanzee habitat, Leakey said. Leakey was intensely interested in these primates, because earlier studies had shown how much chimpanzees were like humans. Leakey mentioned he was looking for someone willing to make a serious study of chimp behavior. It would not be easy, but such a study could provide important clues about how early hominins lived on those very shores as early as two million years ago.

Looking back on those nightly soliloquies, Goodall later said, "I remember wondering what kind of scientist he would find for such a herculean task."[5] By the end of September, at the end

Mary and Louis Leakey became mentors to Goodall.

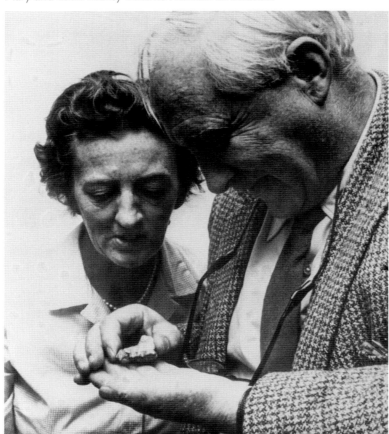

SCIENCE
SPOTLIGHT

LEAKEY'S THEORIES

Louis Leakey was certain that modern humans had not evolved directly from apes, as many other scientists believed. He was convinced humankind and living apes had evolved millions of years ago from a common, ape-like ancestor. Among Louis and Mary Leakey's discoveries were the two-million-year-old remains of creatures that resembled modern humans, or *Homo sapiens*. But the creatures differed, too, in a number of ways. For instance, they were shorter, at only 3.5 to 4 feet (110–120 cm) tall, and they weighed only approximately 70 pounds (32 kg). They also had smaller brains and larger teeth and jaws. One of the creatures, which they called *Australopithecus*, shared similar facial features to humans and walked on two feet in an upright posture. Another creature the Leakeys found the following year consisted of fossils that appeared even more humanlike.

Buried near both creatures, the Leakeys found many pieces of stone tools and a few pieces of utilized bone. They concluded the stones were made and used by the second hominin because it had a bigger brain and humanlike hand. Because of this, they named the second species *Homo habilis*, or "handy man." These findings also helped support Leakey's theory that later *Homo sapiens* first appeared in Africa.

of her season's work at Olduvai, Goodall could think of nothing else. She was convinced she was born to do the chimp study, and one night she told Leakey exactly that. He was delighted. He admitted he'd been waiting for her to ask for the job. His lectures had been sales pitches trying to convince her to do it.

A NEW OPPORTUNITY

Finding money for the new Gombe chimp project was not easy. Goodall had several strikes against her from the point of view of most scientific organizations of the time. First, she was a woman. Established wisdom of the era claimed women were too weak in mind and body for field studies, particularly ones that required long periods alone in isolated, dangerous places. Second, Goodall was young and had no college degree or formal scientific training.

Leakey saw these as advantages, not problems. He believed conventional research methods of the

Women in Primatology

Women scientists had few opportunities in the first half of the 1900s, particularly in the field of primatology, the study of primate behavior. Even so, some women did contribute to pioneer primate studies. On Louis Leakey's advice, Rosalie Osborn, a secretary, and Jill Donisthorpe, a journalist, traveled separately to the Virunga Mountains of East Africa to observe mountain gorillas in their natural habitat in 1956 and 1957. Their close observations and notations were extraordinary for their time. Ideas about what women could and could not do changed dramatically in the 1960s. Jane Goodall and others began breaking into previously all-male fields of study. Today, according to writer Londa Schiebinger, women receive nearly 80 percent of primatology PhDs granted each year.[6]

Trimates

Louis Leakey did a great deal to help women break into the previously all-male field of primate studies, working to advance the careers of Jane Goodall, Dian Fossey, and Biruté Galdikas. He called the women his three primates, or "trimates."[7] All three women made significant contributions to primate research. With Leakey's help, Fossey founded the Karisoke Research Center in Rwanda's Virunga Mountains in 1967. She studied mountain gorillas there for 20 years and wrote a popular book, *Gorillas in the Mist*, about her work. She was murdered in Rwanda in 1985.

Leakey also sponsored the career of Biruté Galdikas, who studied orangutans in the forests of Borneo, Indonesia. She worked tirelessly to protect orangutans and conserve their fragile habitat in Southeast Asia. A university professor, she is today considered the world's leading authority on orangutans.

time were far too cold and clinical. He thought untrained female researchers were exactly what the field of ethology needed. With minds unclouded by preconceived ideas or hypotheses based on what others had already seen and done, they would be able to make more honest observations. Leakey also believed women would be more patient in carrying out tedious fieldwork than men. And he thought animals might accept a woman's presence more readily than a man's because he believed men were more aggressive by nature. From what he had seen of Goodall, Leakey thought she had all of the qualities necessary for the project.

Funding for the program finally appeared. Leighton Wilkie, an American businessman, contributed the money and supplies for the first six months of the Gombe chimp project. After that, the National Geographic Society became the main sponsor of Goodall's continued research.

In letters to family and friends, Goodall often referred to Louis Leakey as her "FFF," short for "Fairy Foster Father."[8] She was sincerely grateful for his faith in her. Yet, both she and Leakey fully understood that his encouragement and support were not offered simply out of kindness. Everything was ultimately about science and the long-range study of wild chimpanzees in their natural habitat.

Leakey believed Goodall's study of modern chimpanzees would strengthen his own theories about early human ancestors. Millions of years ago, humanoid creatures had lived in exactly the same location and environment as chimpanzees lived now. It was up to Goodall to make herself into a working scientist and find the connections between the chimps and humans.

Goodall did more than make herself into a working scientist; she eventually became the world's foremost expert on chimp behavior.

GOMBE

G oodall arrived at Gombe on July 14, 1960, accompanied by her mother. The local British government had demanded that Goodall have a companion with her at Gombe, preferably a female one. Goodall's mother, Vanne, volunteered and stayed at Gombe for five months.

During that time, mother and daughter shared a tent, malaria, and all of the frustrations and uncertainties of exploration. Vanne Goodall, an accomplished writer herself, served as Jane's secretary and assistant. In addition to working on a book of her own, Vanne transcribed notes, wrote letters, and collected insect and plant specimens for her daughter. She also set up a medical clinic at Gombe for local villagers. The clinic mostly dispensed aspirin and bandaged cuts, but Vanne's

As Goodall began her work in Gombe, she couldn't have imagined that she'd soon be touching the chimps she came to study.

A Mother's Support

Goodall always gave her mother credit for the support she provided. She once wrote:

> How lucky I was to have a mother like Vanne—a mother in a million. I could not have done without her during those early days. She ran the [medical] clinic and ensured the goodwill of my neighbors, she kept the camp neat, she pressed and dried for me the specimens of the chimps' food plants that I collected, and, above all, she helped me keep up my spirits during those depressing weeks when I could get nowhere near the chimps. . . . Vanne put up with the most primitive conditions without a murmur.[2]

warm personality and caring attitude greatly improved relations with local people.

Although the early days were emotionally frustrating and physically challenging, in many ways, Goodall had never been happier. She felt that everything she'd done in her life up to this point had foreshadowed and prepared her for this.

Goodall established a daily routine that rarely changed. She rose at dawn, had a slice of bread and a cup of coffee, and then set out to find the chimps. "I never felt the need for food, and seldom for water when I was roaming forests," she wrote later in her book *In the Shadow of Man*.[1] She would stay out all day, and sometimes all night, watching and following chimps, taking notes on small pieces of paper she could easily carry in her pocket. To save space, she devised a tiny scrawl, a kind of shorthand only she could read. When she returned to camp, she transcribed her scribbles into readable script.

Located in eastern Africa, just south of the equator, temperatures at Gombe rarely dip below 60 degrees Fahrenheit (16°C).

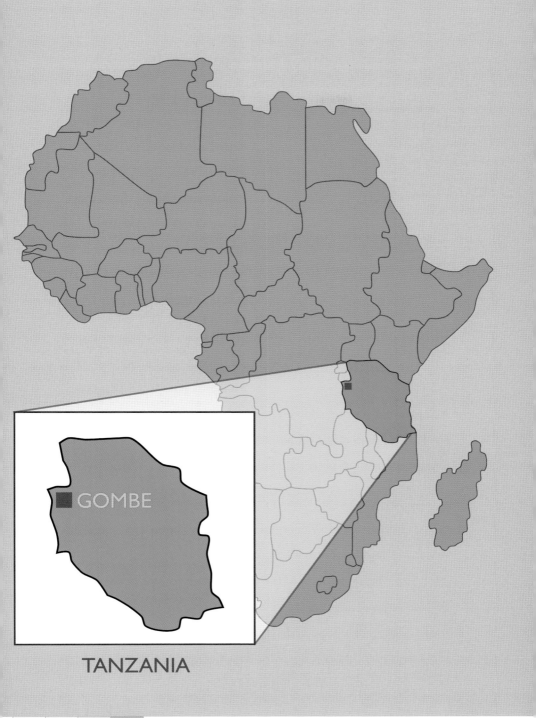

GOMBE

TANZANIA

Rain Dance

Goodall was enchanted one day to see a group of chimps performing what looked like a dance routine during a thunderstorm. It started after a loud clap of thunder and flash of lightning. One chimp suddenly stood upright and began swaying from side to side, calling rhythmically with loud hoots. Other chimps soon joined in, calling together in time, madly swinging around tree trunks, and running and dancing together for nearly half an hour. Goodall later saw similar displays near waterfalls. "With a display and vigor such as this," she said, "primitive man himself might have challenged the elements."[4]

THE TEST

The thrill of her first promising contact with David Graybeard faded as Goodall's first full season at Gombe continued. During this period, Goodall began to sense a change in the chimps' general attitude toward her. It was not a positive one.

For several months, most of the chimps had appeared ready to accept her presence. Many days, they had allowed her to approach and sit near them. Even those who didn't let her get close permitted her to watch and jot notes on their activities.

All of that changed one day when a large chimp Goodall called Goliath suddenly charged at her, teeth bared, hair bristling, mouth open as it let out a ferocious scream. Goodall later described it as "one of the most savage sounds in the African forest."[3] She was terrified but instinctively did not move. Goliath stamped and slapped the ground near her, fixing her with a glaring gaze. He climbed a tree and stood over her, howling and shaking down showers of leaves and branches. One branch broke off and hit her on the head. When she dared to look up, Goliath and the other chimps had vanished.

Aggressive displays by Goliath and other chimps continued for the next several months. It was as if some signal had been passed, Goodall believed. All of the chimps, even David Graybeard, kept their distance, except to leap suddenly from the undergrowth and rush at her, screaming. Chimps sometimes slapped or hit her and threw rocks and other objects.

In addition to having large, ferocious-looking teeth, chimps are incredibly strong—male chimps are twice as strong as male humans.

Throughout the harassment, Goodall did not change her daily routine. She continued to move calmly and slowly through the forest every day, approaching groups of chimps openly and never hiding or surprising them.

Then, one day in 1961, as she approached a fig tree where several chimps had been feeding, she saw two males sitting on the ground grooming one another. When she came closer, she recognized Goliath and David Graybeard. They looked at her for a moment, then calmly returned to their grooming. A few weeks later, Goodall came upon a young male, a short-tempered young chimp she had named Mike. He glanced casually over his shoulder at her before moving away. Soon, even mother chimps with small babies that had never come close before began appearing with regularity.

Her test was over, Goodall decided, and she had passed. What she had accomplished was virtually unprecedented. No one had ever succeeded, in such a short period, in gaining the acceptance and trust of a group of wild primates. Now her real work could begin.

NEW METHODS

After Goodall's first year at Gombe, the hard-earned trust she had developed with the Gombe chimps became a kind of close working relationship. She continued to follow them, but soon even that became somewhat unnecessary. One day, David Graybeard walked directly into Goodall's camp and accepted bananas she tossed onto the ground. Other chimps soon followed, and they kept coming on a regular basis. Suddenly, Goodall was able to watch their social interactions in the open at her camp, without having to hike for miles through the forest.

Chimp Nests

In her early months in Gombe, Goodall was excited to see chimps building nests in trees. She was amazed by the ease and speed with which they broke, folded, and wove together branches and twigs into a sturdy, leafy mat, often within two or three minutes. The chimps at Gombe weighed approximately 80 to 100 pounds (36–45 kg), yet their nests easily supported one or more of them for a night's sleep. Early in her research, Goodall climbed a tree and stretched out on one of the newly vacated nests, finding it free of urine and feces and comfortable, much like a springy mattress.

The chimps' new availability also allowed close filming by Hugo van Lawick, a wildlife photographer sent by the National Geographic Society in August 1962 to capture the amazing things Goodall was reporting. Goodall was thrilled to have someone around who shared her passion for animals. Best of all, van Lawick understood from the start the importance of recording the chimps' every move and gesture. Within weeks of van Lawick's arrival, the chimps accepted his presence, too.

To keep the chimps coming into camp, Goodall and van Lawick began provisioning, a program that involved feeding the chimps bananas, nuts, eggs, and other foods they craved. Supplying wild creatures with food to lure them closer for easier study was not a new idea. But the method presented possible risks. One of the drawbacks of provisioning was that it created an atmosphere of intense competition and tension among the chimps. Things got even worse when Gombe's resident baboons arrived at camp at the same time the chimps were there. At times, the camp was the scene of ferocious battles that flattened tents, damaged equipment, injured animals, and threatened humans.

Provisioning Safety

When provisioning led to violent fights among the animals, Goodall and van Lawick built a steel cage where they could take shelter and keep filming during the fights. Later, they reduced such fights by making major adjustments in the feeding schedule and method. They fed the animals much less frequently. They also moved feeding stations away from camp and constructed special in-ground boxes they could open and close remotely. Feeding could be shut down if things got out of hand and restarted when peace was restored.

Despite the risks, provisioning provided the opportunity to get dramatic new insights into chimp behavior and society. Soon after the provisioning experiment started, Goodall wrote in a letter to Louis Leakey, "The results I am getting now are the sort of things I never dreamed of getting."[5]

Previously, while watching the animals in the thick brush, Goodall had seen only individuals or small groups of chimps.

With the promise of food, the chimps were eager to come into Goodall's camp, giving her a chance to study them up close.

Observing large numbers of chimps interacting with one another gave her an entirely different perspective. She began to recognize family relationships and the important role of dominance and submission in chimp society. As she had with David Graybeard, she now began to identify and name other chimps and record their many physical and personality differences. Like humans, chimps displayed a wide array of interests, temperaments, and intelligence. They were all different, she realized.

Goodall also began to see evidence of emotions she identified as sadness, joy, jealousy, and perhaps even love. Goodall understood that saying animals other than humans were capable of such complex feelings set her apart from most scientists of her time. Yet, she could not ignore what she was seeing. She was convinced chimpanzees were far more like

SCIENCE
SPOTLIGHT

ETHOLOGY IN THE MID-1960S

The study of animals in their natural habitats is known as ethology. Yet, when Goodall began her research, many ethologists studied primates in laboratories. Robert Yerkes, a leading ethologist from the 1920s to the 1950s, thought of chimps mainly as laboratory research subjects that could be experimented on and used to improve human lives. Similarly, in the 1960s, Harry Harlow received the United States' most prestigious science award, the National Medal of Science, for his psychological research with rhesus monkeys. All of his experiments were performed in the laboratory, and many of them subjected animals to physical and psychological pain.

Overlooked and almost forgotten by the 1960s was the work of Konrad Lorenz. Even though he was still working in the 1960s, Lorenz's methods and approaches were considered old-fashioned and unscientific. He emphasized the importance of studying animal behavior in the wild, not in the laboratory. He believed that only long hours of intensive observation in the wild could reveal an animal's individual differences and provide insights into humans. Although Lorenz's methods stood in opposition to what was considered credible science at the time, they strongly influenced Goodall, who adopted them in her own work.

humans than anyone had ever suspected. After one particularly enlightening day with her chimps in 1963, Goodall noted, "I used to think I knew at any rate something about them. I now know that I knew next to nothing. They cannot be thought of as animals—they just cannot."[6]

A NEED FOR MORE EDUCATION

In 1989, scientist and historian Stephen Jay Gould would write that Goodall's research "will rank forever as one of the great achievements of scientific dedication, combined with stunning results."[7] In the early 1960s, however, the scientific community was not yet ready to take Goodall or her work seriously.

One of the biggest things holding her work back from scientific recognition was her lack of academic credentials. Her only real educational accomplishment to date was a high school diploma from Uplands School for Girls. Based on Leakey's strong recommendation, however, in 1962 Cambridge University in England accepted Goodall into its graduate program in animal behavior.

For the next three years, Goodall spent half of each year at Cambridge working toward her doctoral degree. She found it agonizing to leave her chimps, but she knew acceptance of her work depended upon a piece of paper and the letters *PhD* after her name.

CHAPTER
FIVE

BECOMING
A SCIENTIST

G oodall's first article appeared in the summer of 1963 in
National Geographic magazine. Writing in the engaging
narrative style that would become her trademark, Goodall
essentially told the story of her first year at Gombe. In a sidebar,
Leonard Carmichael, secretary of the Smithsonian Institution,
commented on Goodall's courage in facing alone such "powerful
and potentially dangerous animals." He added, "It is thus
possible that the interesting account given here will stand for
all time as a unique record in scientific zoological literature."[1]
Accompanying photos taken by Hugo van Lawick showed a thin,
petite young woman, her hair pulled back in a tight ponytail,
smiling whimsically at chimps. The article was a huge popular

People around the world were amazed by Goodall's accounts
of her life among the chimps of Gombe.

success. Goodall received the National Geographic Society's Franklin Burr Award for outstanding contributions to science.

Despite the popular acclaim, Goodall's text didn't impress some scientists, who found the article's cute pictures and charming style unscientific. Rumors circulated that perhaps her discoveries had been faked and even that Goodall had taught chimps how to make and use tools. Some ethologists sharply criticized Goodall's use of provisioning, saying that it manipulated chimps into unnatural social behavior.

Nonverbal Communication

One day in October 1964, Goodall followed David Graybeard through the forest. At some point, he stopped and, according to Goodall, seemed to wait for her. She and the chimp "sat and ate leaves side by side" for a while, she later wrote.[2] Then Goodall saw a ripe palm nut on the ground, picked it up, and held it out to him, something she had never done before. David eyed the food a moment before he turned away. Goodall persisted, holding the nut even closer and almost touching him. A moment later, David turned suddenly and took her hand with the nut still in it. For nearly ten seconds, he held her hand. He took the nut, looked at it a moment, then dropped it to the ground. Goodall called the experience "the most significant of my life."[3] She wrote:

The soft pressure of his fingers spoke to me not through my intellect but through a more primitive emotional channel: the barrier of untold centuries which has grown up during the separate evolution of man and chimpanzee was for those few seconds, broken down.[4]

She later said this was the moment when she first knew that chimps and humans shared a common ancestor.

Many of the attacks that dismissed Goodall's work as amateurish and unscientific were based on thinly disguised prejudice. Many scientists believed that a woman had no business doing field research. After Goodall presented her first paper at a scientific convention, Zoological Society of London chairman Sir Solly Zuckerman commented that her work was just "glamor parading as science."[5]

Goodall's research methods were often called into question as well. She did not follow the scientific method. She was not framing scientific questions and testing hypotheses with observational or experimental evidence. What conclusion did she hope to draw? Her work was based on no particular theory, many claimed. Goodall pointed out that this was incorrect. She had set out to prove that chimpanzee behavior in the wild echoes human behavior, particularly that of humankind's earliest ancestors. She also wanted to prove her deeply held convictions that "animals had personalities; that they could feel happy or sad or fearful; that they could feel pain; that they could strive towards planned goals."[6] But few of her colleagues at that time were ready to listen.

One thing Goodall could not argue against, however, was that she was emotionally involved with her subjects. Critics said she could not be objective if she cared so deeply. She touched chimps, played with them, fed them, and even referred to them in reports as her friends. She gave them cute names, instead of impersonal numbers, as other primate behaviorists did. "I readily admit to a high level of emotional involvement with individual chimpanzees," Goodall said.[7] But a deep emotional connection with her subjects was the cornerstone of her research method. Such trust was exactly what allowed her

Despite the criticism of other scientists, Goodall formed close relationships with the chimps she studied.

access to chimps' most intimate behavior. For years, this issue remained one of the most divisive points of contention between Goodall and her colleagues.

EARNING HER DEGREE

Robert Hinde, Goodall's academic adviser at Cambridge and a leading figure in primate ethology at the time, was initially dissatisfied with the narrative approach of her writing. He did not hide his disappointment with the 850 pages Goodall turned in as the first draft of her doctoral thesis. He said the paper was just charming stories and vivid descriptions. Worse, it contained conclusions based on feelings and intuition and lacked hard facts. Student and adviser had lengthy arguments regarding her methods and her dissertation. Other Cambridge professors held Goodall's work up as a model of what not to do.

Even so, Goodall and her chimps had become enormously popular with the general public. The National Geographic Society had begun making films about Goodall, introducing her and her chimps to millions of people around the world. Her growing fame in the United States and Europe, not to mention her support by the National Geographic Society and Louis Leakey, eventually made it almost impossible for Cambridge to deny Goodall her PhD in ethology, and she received the degree in 1966.

Speaking years later about her early struggles for acceptance, Goodall said, "I didn't give two hoots for what they thought. They were wrong, and I was right."[8] The only thing that truly mattered to her was getting back to Gombe and her beloved chimps. Her feelings about them and the work she was doing had not changed. "My own ultimate goal has always been that out of a thorough understanding of chimpanzee behavior should come a furthering of our understanding of our own behavior," she said.[9]

"But now—now life is so wonderful. The challenge has been met. The hills & forests are my home. And what is more, I think my mind works like a chimp's, subconsciously."[10]

—Jane Goodall, letter to her family, July 14, 1961

DEEPER INSIGHTS

At the urging of Robert Hinde, in 1968, Goodall published her doctoral dissertation, "Behaviour of Free-living Chimpanzees in the Gombe Stream Reserve," in the scientific journal *Animal Behaviour*. It was the first scholarly presentation of her Gombe chimp research.

As Goodall's scientific reputation grew, so did the Gombe Stream Research Centre. It expanded rapidly in the late 1960s and early 1970s. In 1967, Gombe became a Tanzanian national park, which meant greater support and protection for workers and chimps. In September 1968, the primate studies program at Stanford University in California began sending American student assistants to work and study at Gombe. By 1972, more than 100 people, including students and African staff members and their families, were living at the research center.[11]

The additional help and company offered both positives and negatives for Goodall. She now spent more time doing paperwork and mentoring students than she spent monitoring chimps. She missed the quiet isolation and one-to-one contact with the animals. Still, the days of crude tents and loneliness were over. Gombe Research Centre became a small village with work buildings, offices, and dorms. Goodall learned to use student assistants' hands and eyes as tools. The key to field research is accumulating a large amount of data, and her assistants sped up the process. As Goodall said, "the spirit of Gombe" was all about sharing.[12] Every day, Goodall and her energetic group of assistants saw and learned things no one had ever seen or known about chimps before.

This faster accumulation of information allowed Goodall to see how the behavior of individual chimps fit together into a pattern. Deeper insights helped her form a picture of how chimp society worked. Goodall came to understand that the 50 to 100 chimps she had been studying were members of one cohesive northern community.[13] The place and role of each chimp in that close-knit social group were determined by

Dung Swirling

A great deal of what wild chimps eat passes through their system undigested. Goodall used this fact to collect data about the Gombe chimps' diet. She and her assistants carried bags and collected huge amounts of chimp droppings wherever they went. To study it, they put the dung into shallow pans with a little water and swirled it, like prospectors panning for gold. Examining the solid residue left in the bottom gave a clear picture of what particular chimps ate.

specific rules based largely on dominance interactions. The periodically explosive and violent displays by male chimps, which terrorized and sometimes even injured others, were power displays. The social order demanded that the strongest, most vocal individual would be the alpha male, or leader. All the other chimps in the community, from the strongest to the weakest, had to show submission to chimps above them in the social order.

As Goodall began figuring out the complex system of alliances and relationships that helped sustain balance in chimp society, she also identified gestures and expressions individuals used to signal their place in the social order. She described gestures of greeting, calming, and playing that proved to her that chimps genuinely liked and cared for one another. She observed chimps almost constantly touching one another with gentle pats, tickles, hand-holding, kisses, and hugs. She identified social grooming as one of the most frequent reassuring behaviors chimps exhibited. This involved one animal rubbing and picking at another animal's fur. Goodall knew the gesture was partially hygienic, to clean coats of insects and dirt, but she believed it was even more important as a calming and relaxing behavior.

THE IMPORTANCE OF FAMILY

Through her observations, Goodall also identified family units. She noted the strong influence mothers had on offspring, even into their adulthood, and she became especially fascinated by Flo, the highest-ranking female chimp at Gombe. Flo and her family became the focus of a great deal of the work Goodall and her assistants did. Goodall's team followed Flo for approximately ten years. They tracked her offspring even longer, for an estimated total of 40,000 hours of observations.[14]

Flo had been one of the first female chimps to approach Goodall in her early days at Gombe. Goodall first described her as "the most hideous old bag in Chimpland" and said Flo looked like a "prehistoric stone age woman," with her small, skinny, crooked body, spindly legs, bulbous nose, and drooping lower lip.[15] But Goodall soon learned that despite her odd appearance, Flo was the most desired female at Gombe. Records showed she mated more often than any other female. Watching Flo allowed Goodall to learn more about chimp mating and motherhood than anyone before her. She learned that, unlike other primates such as gorillas, baboons, and humans, female chimps often mate with many males. She also discovered that chimp mothers and babies form a strong bond that lasts even after the young chimps leave their mother at age four or five.

Watching Flo and her baby became even more special for Goodall later. She and Hugo van Lawick had married in the spring of 1964, and they began thinking about starting a family. Goodall was so impressed by the devotion and care chimp mothers showed for their infants, she decided that she would model herself after them and raise her baby the same way. In her book *In the Shadow of Man*, Goodall later wrote, "Flo taught me to honor the role of the mother in society and to appreciate

Mother chimps give birth only once every five years and usually have only one baby at a time.

not only the importance to a child of good mothering, but also the joy and contentment which that relationship can bring to the mother."[16]

Goodall ultimately came to believe that chimp society was based more firmly on family ties, with the role of mothers at the center, than on any other force, including male dominance. This belief led Goodall, after her first decade of research, to conclude that chimp society was in many ways superior to human society. Goodall pointed this out in her first book, titled *My Friends the Wild Chimpanzees*, which was published in 1967. In this children's book, she suggested chimps were friendlier, kinder, and less-hostile creatures than modern humans. During this early period, some of her assumptions were still based on intuitive feelings she'd had about her dog Rusty and animals in general since she was a small child. As time passed and she collected and recorded more behavioral data, however, Goodall's ideas about chimps' essential goodness would change.

A Fission-Fusion Society

Goodall found that the main Gombe chimpanzee community was a fission-fusion society. This means that not all members of the group remain together all the time. Individual chimps of both sexes frequently drifted from one small social cluster to another. So, chimps were familiar with a great many different individuals but didn't see or socialize with all of them every day. This flexible and open type of social organization is unusual among nonhuman primates, such as baboons, which usually live in smaller, closed social groups.

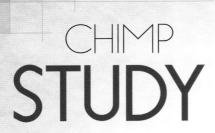

CHIMP
STUDY

GESTURES AND EXPRESSIONS

Among the many discoveries Jane Goodall made about chimpanzee behavior was the important role gestures and facial expressions play in communication and social interaction.

Calm and contented chimps keep their mouths closed or slightly open with lips relaxed. When they are worried or afraid, many chimps form the pout face, lips extended, and make a soft *woo-woo* sound. The play face—mouth open, teeth not exposed— is usually made while laughing, which chimps do a great deal. Fear or distress might be signaled by a closed-tooth grin, with lips half closed. Or a chimp might make a *haa* sound through a partly open grin, with sharp teeth exposed.

Body language is important, too. Reaching out a limp hand serves as a sign of greeting, while flinging one arm with an open palm high over the head is a sign of aggression or threat. Squatting or sitting is a calm posture. Standing on all fours, especially while leaning forward, rocking, or bouncing signals extreme anger or agitation.

Goodall became so good at chimp speak, she could imitate many of the animals' sounds and gesture. She often startled audiences by beginning speeches with a loud *pant-hoot* sound.

CALM AND
CONTENTED

FEAR OR
DISTRESS

PLAY FACE

WORRIED OR AFRAID
POUT FACE

DANGEROUS DAYS

One day in September 1966, a mother chimp named Olly arrived at the provisioning area with her new baby. The infant was screaming and appeared unable to cling to Olly as she moved. The horrible screaming alerted everyone in camp, and Goodall scribbled in her notes that the baby appeared to be "quite paralyzed."[1] The next morning, the infant was dead. A short time later, another chimp was seen with one arm dangling and useless. The list of chimp casualties grew quickly. Observers reported stiff necks, bent and disabled arms, and crippled hands, feet, and legs. David Graybeard showed up at camp one day unable to put weight on one leg.

The diagnosis soon became clear. Polio had stricken a number of people in villages near Gombe, and the disease had

Goodall interacts with a chimp for the CBS TV special *Miss Goodall and the World of Chimpanzees*, which aired in 1965.

spread to the chimps. Shipments of oral polio vaccine soon arrived at Gombe. Goodall and van Lawick began dosing the human staff first. They then administered the vaccine to as many chimps as possible by putting drops of vaccine into bananas. It was too late to save them all, however. "The whole affair has been like living in a nightmare," Goodall wrote to a friend in mid-December.[2] Chimps still kept turning up with crippled arms and legs, and several died. By the time the polio epidemic finally ended in January 1967, it had claimed the lives of four chimps and left five others with partial paralysis. A flu epidemic that swept through Gombe a year later claimed several more of Goodall's favorite chimps, including her first chimp friend, David Graybeard. Goodall felt an enormous sense of sadness and loss at the death of some of her closest chimp friends.

GRUB

Yet, her sorrow was eased a great deal by the arrival of her own healthy son, Hugo Eric Louis van Lawick, on March 4, 1967. From the start, his mother called him Grub. Goodall still intended to raise Grub as much as possible the way a chimp mother would. That meant providing constant attention and lots of cuddling, playing, and touching for at least his first two years. Grub never spent a single night away from his mother until he was three years old.

SCIENCE
SPOTLIGHT

GOMBE CHIMPS
AND AIDS PREVENTION

Polio is not the only deadly disease that affects chimps. Using the same detailed data collection procedures pioneered by Jane Goodall, student researchers at Gombe Stream continue to study the health of chimpanzees today. They're looking for signs of simian immunodeficiency virus (SIV), the virus that led to the acquired immunodeficiency syndrome (AIDS) pandemic in humans.

Similar to their role model, the students spend many long hours following chimps through the rugged, brushy landscape. In this case, though, they study the chimps' physical behavior mainly to watch for signs of illness. For years, researchers have observed chimps to set standards of good and poor health. This analysis has determined that infectious disease is the leading cause of death in wild chimps. Clearly ill chimps are closely monitored, and feces samples are tested to determine if the sickness is SIV.

Elizabeth Lonsdorf, assistant professor of psychology at Franklin and Marshall College in Lancaster, Pennsylvania, and director of the study, said the project provides invaluable information that will eventually help medical researchers find a way to stop the spread of SIV to humans. But just as important, Lonsdorf said, "We want to do everything we can to prevent chimpanzee population declines."[3]

Almost from the start, Grub did not like chimps and had occasional nightmares about them. People in neighboring villages reported that chimps had snatched and eaten babies. As a precaution, Grub's parents had protective metal mesh installed on the windows and even had a steel cage installed for Grub to sleep in.

Grub, the Bush Baby

Goodall assembled a scrapbook of photos of Grub as a toddler to give as a Christmas gift to the boy's two grandmothers. When publisher Billy Collins visited Goodall and van Lawick at Gombe to discuss books they were working on, he happened to see the scrapbook. He told Goodall, "I must publish this. It's marvelous!"[4] The result was the 1970 children's book *Grub the Bush Baby*, with text by Goodall and photos by van Lawick.

Still, when he was old enough, Grub was allowed to play in the lake and along the shore. By the time he was seven, Grub developed a special love for the water— swimming, boating, and fishing. It would remain his lifelong passion. He enjoyed trips into the forest, too, as long as his parents were there to protect him. Just like Flo's babies, Grub loved rough-and-tumble play and adored being swung upside down by the ankles. As he grew older, he had a few brushes with disaster, including close encounters with poisonous snakes, wild baboons, and shrieking chimps.

Perhaps one of Grub's biggest hurdles was the separation of his parents as their careers took them in different directions.

Goodall and her son Grub on the shores of Lake Tanganyika

Van Lawick's work took him to the Serengeti, while Goodall remained at Gombe.

VIOLENT DISPLAYS

During her time at Gombe, Goodall had observed chimps eating meat and performing violent dominance displays. Yet, she had held on to her basic assumption that chimps were, as she wrote, "for the most part, rather nicer than human beings."[5]

Her opinion changed dramatically during the first few years of the 1970s. Events at Gombe forced her to reconsider her

Mike's Bluff

Mike was a small but exceptionally clever and curious chimp. One day, he found some large discarded kerosene cans. He quickly discovered that banging the empty tin cans together made a terrific racket. A short time later, Goodall watched Mike hide the cans in the brush near a well-traveled path. He sat down and waited until a group of high-ranking males approached. Among them was Goliath, the largest and most powerful chimp at Gombe. Mike slipped quietly into the bushes.

A few moments later, he burst into the open, rolling the cans in front of him and screaming with all his might. Terrified by the thunderous noise and motion, the larger males ran for cover.

Mike used the cans as tools of terror several times before Goodall took them away. By that time, though, Mike's social status had changed. Even without his noisemakers, whenever Mike displayed dominance, chimps scattered. Even Goliath approached him warily, making gestures of submission and respect. "Thus," Goodall wrote, "small but smart Mike became in 1964 the top-ranking male of Gombe," with first choice of food and mates.[6] He remained in power for the next six years.

Goodall's hut had metal over the windows to keep potentially dangerous chimps out.

somewhat rosy image of chimps as humankind's more peaceful relative. As she wrote, "There is a great deal in chimpanzee social relations to remind us of some of our own behavior; more, perhaps, than many of us care to admit."[7]

Starting in 1972, Goodall and her assistants witnessed an increase in violence between two Gombe groups. Chimps in a group from the northern Kasekela Valley engaged in coordinated raids and battles against a smaller southern group from the Kahama Valley.

The growing level of violence disturbed Goodall. She could explain some of the conflicts as clashes over territory. But she found it harder to understand the sheer savagery of many of the attacks. The apparent delight the winners exhibited while murdering and frequently cannibalizing members of their own species troubled Goodall. "Suddenly," she wrote, "we found that chimpanzees could be brutal—that they, like us, had a dark side to their nature."[8]

She even worried that she might be witnessing a terrible step in chimpanzee evolution. As she wrote:

> The chimpanzee . . . has clearly reached a stage where he stands at the very threshold of human achievement in destruction. If ever he develops the power of language . . . might he not push open the door and wage war with the best of us?[9]

Goodall discussed some of her ideas about chimps' darker side in her book *In the Shadow of Man,* which appeared in 1971 to critical and popular acclaim. According to Goodall's biographer, Dale Peterson, Goodall's "unique personality and distinctive writing style" were on full display in this work.[10] The book featured adventure, danger, and suspense alongside pure

Teddy Boys

Early on, Goodall noticed the tendency of chimp males to form alliances, which she called a sort of "gang warfare system."[11] One day, she saw a group of somewhat weaker males join forces against Goliath, the powerful alpha male. Acting together, they drove him away from food they wanted for themselves. Goodall called the chimp gang "teddy boys," a British expression for young gang members or juvenile delinquents.[12]

science, presenting Goodall's "astonishing discovery of intelligent life beyond our own," as Peterson wrote.[13] Peterson said that *In the Shadow of Man* placed Goodall squarely "at the heart of the new science of primate-watching" and "significantly contributed to Jane's popular reputation as a scientist."[14] A short time after her book's appearance, Goodall was elected to the American Academy of Arts and Sciences, a society that recognizes achievements in several fields, including science. In a letter home, she admitted she did not know exactly what the election meant but said that she felt "fearfully honored."[15] Despite the recognition, Goodall faced darker days ahead.

Poor Flo

In 1972, Flo, the highest-ranking female of the Gombe community, was ill and showing her age. In a letter home, Goodall described "poor Flo," who was then 40 or 50 years old, as "quite literally, a skeleton with some hairy flesh around it."[16] A short time later, Flo was found dead in the forest. Within weeks, Flo's eight-year-old son, whom Goodall described as depressed, died, too. Grief-stricken, Goodall wrote an obituary for Flo that appeared along with a photo in the London *Sunday Times*. "I owe her a personal debt of gratitude," Goodall wrote in the obituary. "For me, Gombe can never be quite the same."[17]

CHAPTER SEVEN

OMENS OF CHANGE

In 1973, Goodall met and fell in love with Derek Bryceson, a British war hero and director of Tanzania's national parks. For a while, Goodall was miserable, torn between her desire to marry Bryceson and concerns over how van Lawick and her son, Grub, would react if she asked for a divorce.

In January 1974, Goodall, Grub, and Bryceson flew in a small plane from the Tanzanian capital Dar es Salaam for a short visit to remote Ruaha National Park in central Tanzania. As the plane prepared to land, the pilot lost control, and the plane crashed into the rugged African countryside. Incredibly, no one was seriously hurt.

Goodall's life with the chimps would undergo major changes in the 1970s.

Shortly afterward, Goodall wrote to her family, saying that the accident "is like an omen and I feel quite strange about it."[1] The crash was a spiritual turning point for Goodall, who wrote, "Lots of things seem to have fallen into shape after nearly being dead—you know, you suddenly realize that it could happen (death, I mean) at any moment. So [you think about] what is best to do with the life entrusted to you."[2] Later that year, Goodall and van Lawick officially divorced, and in January 1975, she married Bryceson. She remained at Gombe, while he lived in Dar es Salaam, where he worked. The two traveled back and forth frequently.

By now, Goodall's fame and reputation were soaring, and she found life and work at Gombe increasingly hectic. In exchange for American students working as assistants at Gombe, Goodall agreed to spend a few months each year as a visiting professor at Stanford University in California. Traveling and living abroad were hard, and time away from her family and her chimps was even worse. She often felt lonely, weary, and restless.

CHIMP WAR

Goodall also continued struggling with the realization that chimps were not the perfectly peaceful creatures she had believed them to be. The dark side of the chimps' nature erupted in 1974 in a long and bloody territorial war between the

SCIENCE
SPOTLIGHT

FIELD RESEARCH

Ethological field procedure involves four basic steps: finding animals, getting close enough to actually see what they are doing, recording their behavior, and analyzing the collected data. Prior to Goodall's work, ethologists struggled to get past the second step. In fact, despite repeated attempts to study wild chimpanzees, no one had been able to figure out how to do it.

Goodall's nonconfrontational approach opened the door. Presenting herself to the chimps and allowing them to decide if they would accept her was the key. They were always in control. That approach forever changed the way ethologists did field research.

Another innovation of Goodall's research involved the third step. Her Cambridge mentor, Robert Hinde, suggested she create checklists of specific behaviors instead of scribbling random notes. These standardized charts allowed Goodall and her assistants to more easily and quickly record what individual chimps were doing. For instance, when a chimp ate something, they only had to check *eating* on the checklist and record the time and what was eaten. Checklists became the primary tool of ethological field research at Gombe and made the next step, data collection and analysis, possible.

Goodall was the first person to record warfare among nonhuman primates.

northern and southern groups of chimps. The attacks went on for several years, until the northern group completely wiped out the southern group.

Even more disturbing to Goodall was the behavior of a mature female, whom Goodall named Passion, and her adolescent daughter, Pom. Goodall had been observing the two female chimps for some time. She had once described Passion as "a somewhat unnatural mother."[3] The polar opposite of patient, nurturing Flo, Passion was cold and uncaring toward her baby. She left Pom lying on the ground for long periods, unfed and crying. Passion never cuddled or played with Pom, either. When Passion moved around, she did not pick up Pom and carry her. Instead, the baby had to scramble to catch her mother's fur and hang on for dear life. If she fell off, Passion did not stop. Goodall reasoned that Pom's upbringing led her to grow into a troubled young adult.

In 1974, during the spike in violence between the northern and southern groups, Goodall watched as Passion attacked a new mother chimp named Gilka. During a vicious encounter, Passion ripped Gilka's baby away from her, killed it, and ate it, sharing the meat with Pom. Gilka's new baby was a victim the following year. Six other chimp babies vanished around the same time, all of which Goodall attributed to the reign of terror of Passion and Pom. During the next few years, the terrible incident was repeated. Only one

Nature or Nurture?

Goodall's observations about chimp aggression and warfare added fuel to an already fiery debate in the scientific community. Anthropologists argued among themselves over what caused human wars. Some believed humankind had been nurtured to make war—that is, people had learned how to make war by savage ancestors. In that case, humans might be able to unlearn war-making. But other anthropologists thought nature had given humans an aggression gene that made wars inevitable.

Goodall's chimp studies seemed to prove the latter idea, although she refused to believe it. In fact, convincing people that they could learn how to stop fighting occupied much of her life after her Gombe work ended.

female in the Gombe study group, Flo's daughter Fifi, managed to raise an infant successfully during those years.

RAID ON GOMBE

The violent upheavals in chimp society seemed to mirror the political turmoil occurring among the human population. In Zaire (now the Democratic Republic of the Congo), 25 miles (40 km) across Lake Tanganyika from Tanzania, rebels fought with government forces for control of the nation. In the dead of night on May 19, 1975, armed rebels crossed the lake in boats and stormed ashore at Gombe, near the house where Goodall and Grub were sleeping. The well-armed rebels burst into buildings in the Gombe staff village. They threatened African workers, demanding to know where Goodall was. When the workers would not tell them, the raiders beat them mercilessly. The rebels entered a dorm where student assistants were lodged. Three American students and a Dutch research assistant were kidnapped and taken to a rebel camp in Zaire. Afraid for Goodall's safety, her students and staff woke her to tell her of the kidnappings only after the raid was over.

The rebels issued a statement demanding a ransom in exchange for the captives. If payment was not made, they said, all hostages would be killed. For her own safety, Goodall went to live at her husband's house in Dar es Salaam. For the next three months, American and Tanzanian government officials negotiated the release of the captives. After ransom money was supplied by the students' families, Stanford, and other donors, rebel leaders in Zaire finally released the three American students. They freed the Dutch assistant as a goodwill gesture.

Once the ordeal was over, the Tanzanian government informed Goodall she would not be allowed to return to Gombe. Civil wars and unstable political situations in neighboring African countries made it too dangerous for Europeans and Americans to work in Tanzania. An all-Tanzanian staff, including a new director, was placed in charge of the national park and the primate research center. Most of them

From her home in Dar es Salaam, Goodall wrote 20 to 30 letters a day promoting chimp research and protection efforts.

were people Goodall had trained and worked with before, so she was able to get regular reports and updates. But for the next few years, Goodall was granted permission to return to the park only two or three times and even then, only for brief, nonworking visits. Some questioned whether the chimpanzee research center would remain in operation.

In 1975, when Grub was eight years old, he went to live in England with his grandmother Vanne and her family to finish his schooling there. Goodall remained in Dar es Salaam with her husband, close to Gombe and her chimps. Her career as a primate field researcher was now essentially over. But even if she was no longer the research center's on-site director, the center and its work were still her creation. She was determined to find a way to keep it going. She had to find a reliable source of funding.

In 1977, on the advice of friends, she established the Jane Goodall Institute, a nonprofit foundation. The institute gave Goodall a place to channel all her funds, which included grants, donations, and book revenues. Bryceson was no longer director of Tanzania's national parks, but he still lived and worked in Dar es Salaam and was a friend of many important government officials. He used his connections to rally support for Gombe. Goodall had friends and colleagues working at Gombe as well. They understood her level of commitment to the chimpanzees,

Goodall's Influence on Others

The list of scientists influenced and inspired by Goodall is long. Among them was naturalist Sy Montgomery, who studied emus in Australia using Goodall's approach and methods. What made Goodall's approach different and special, Montgomery said, was "that she relinquished control. Today this strength is honored, not as a passive act, as the men before her might have seen it, but as an achievement."[4]

Another scientist influenced by Goodall was Barbara Smuts, who worked at Gombe for several years while a student in behavioral biology at Stanford. Smuts became interested in the behavior of adult female chimpanzees in the wild and spent several years studying social relationships in wild olive baboons in Kenya and Tanzania. She also studied wild bottlenose dolphins in Western Australia and dog behavior at the University of Michigan.

Geza Teleki worked with Goodall at Gombe for two years and later studied primates in Sierra Leone. Teleki died in 2014, and as a friend pointed out in a memorial tribute, he was like his mentor Jane Goodall because he "thought much more highly of chimpanzees as a species [than he did humans], in fact, and it was this view that motivated his many successful efforts on their behalf."[5]

and they made sure her scientific and advisory role continued, even if it could only be from a distance.

SAD DAYS

In October 1980, Bryceson died of cancer. Goodall spent the winter and spring of 1981 mourning her husband's passing. She remained in Dar es Salaam, working on Gombe business, raising funds, reviewing reports sent by the Tanzanian staff, and trying to cope with her loss.

In May 1981, Goodall was allowed to return to Gombe for a brief visit. It had always been a place of peace and renewal for her. She went into the forest and saw Fifi and other chimps she'd known in happier days past. While she followed a boisterous group, a tremendous storm struck. She hunkered down, chimp-like, with them to wait it out, moving deep into her imagination, as she had always done in times of physical or mental discomfort.

When the rain stopped, the forest was dripping and gorgeous. The chimps were bright and shiny in beams of sunlight. Suddenly, as Goodall wrote in her book *Reason for Hope*, "I and the chimpanzees, the earth and trees and air, seemed to merge, to become one with the spirit power of life itself."[6] She called it a "mystical experience" and a moment of "timelessness and quiet ecstasy."[7] The clouds of gloom inside her lifted. She knew it was time for her to get on with the rest of her life.

Gombe would always be a place of peace for Goodall.

NEW DIRECTIONS

For years, Goodall had thought about publishing the massive accumulation of information, data, stories, notes, and background material she had gathered at Gombe. In 1981, she began the enormous task of organizing it all into a coherent document. This mass of data, she realized, represented her life's work and her contribution to science. Assembling her monograph became the single most important activity in her life. When it was finally published in 1986, *The Chimpanzees of Gombe: Patterns of Behavior* was a complex 650-page scientific work, with photographic documentation, charts, maps, diagrams, tables, and footnotes. It presented more than 25 years of observations of the behavior and ecology of chimpanzees—

After the publication of *Chimpanzees of Gombe*, Goodall found herself in high demand as a speaker.

more detail on the free-ranging behavior of a single species than had ever been compiled.

At the same time, *The Chimpanzees of Gombe* was exceptionally readable for a nonscientific audience. Since childhood, Goodall had always had a gift for explaining and storytelling. Both were on full display in her monograph. As writer Carol Lee Flinders concluded, *The Chimpanzees of Gombe* "proved once and for all to her most distinguished colleagues that the whimsical spinner of tales was also a dedicated, uncompromising scientist."[1] Most scientist reviewers of her book agreed. Cynthia Worsley at the University of Manitoba conducted a survey of reviews of *The Chimpanzees of Gombe*. She found that four scientist reviewers—two biologists, an anthropologist, and a veterinary anatomist—praised Goodall's "attention to detail and the fact that she has proven the value of anecdotal evidence through sustained observation."[2] Worsley also found the scientist reviewers liked "the fact that her work is accessible to the general reader, not just the primatologist."[3]

The extraordinary reception of *The Chimpanzees of Gombe* confirmed Goodall's scientific and literary reputation and secured her financial future. Awards and invitations to speak poured in. Yet, fame and fortune had never been among her personal goals. Now that her book was complete and her fieldwork at Gombe was winding down, Goodall wondered what she should do next.

ANIMAL ACTIVIST

In November 1986, Goodall accepted an invitation to attend a conference on understanding chimpanzees sponsored by the Chicago Academy of Sciences. The event, organized largely as a celebration of *The Chimpanzees of Gombe*, brought primatologists from around the world. As the world's leading expert on chimp behavior, Goodall was the star attraction.

The Chicago conference turned out to be another transformational event in her life. While listening to discussions and presentations on environmental issues and the mistreatment of chimpanzees, Goodall suddenly felt what she later called "a cataclysmic change."[4] She was stunned by the descriptions she heard of the plight of chimpanzees worldwide. She suddenly realized how indifferent she had been to the suffering of animals beyond the borders of Gombe.

ChimpanZoo

In 1984, Goodall launched a project called ChimpanZoo. Its purpose was to improve conditions for chimpanzees in zoos and sanctuaries worldwide. The idea was to educate and motivate people in charge of captive chimps to create humane and natural living spaces. The project was designed to encourage the study and collection of behavioral data in captive environments, using the same methods Goodall had pioneered among wild chimps. Support for this program is still one of the Jane Goodall Institute's most important goals.

FUTURE
TECH

PLAY AS PREPARATION FOR ADULTHOOD

Following methods Goodall originated, researchers are still making new discoveries about chimps. In 2015, a team of researchers led by University of Zurich anthropologist Kathelijne Koops observed young chimps at play. Goodall long ago noted that chimp children like to pick up and play with natural objects. Koops and her colleagues noticed what appeared to be a major difference between how male and female chimps played with these objects.

Boy chimps picked up sticks and rocks and threw them around. They aggressively chased other boy chimps with them. Girl chimps were quieter and more creative. They tended to use items to achieve some goal or as tools or objects of creative play. For instance, young female chimps cradled sticks and laid them in improvised sleeping nests.

It seemed clear to Koops that play for young chimps was preparation for adulthood. Scientists have long known that human children do the same thing. This discovery adds to the long list of ways chimps and humans are similar. It adds support to an original theory shared by Leakey and Goodall that chimps and humans share a common ancestor.

In captivity or in the wild, young chimps find many uses for sticks.

Goodall learned wild chimp populations were rapidly disappearing as human population growth in Africa and Asia destroyed their natural habitat. Hunters in many parts of Africa killed and sold chimpanzees and other wild creatures. This so-called bushmeat trade helped feed hungry people, but it also decimated remaining populations of primates. Chimps were also being captured in growing numbers for pets, for the entertainment industry, and for medical research.

Goodall's connection with chimpanzees would not allow her to sit idly by and do nothing. "I owe it to the chimps," she said simply.[5] That conference inspired the next phase of her life—her work as an environmental activist.

Goodall threw herself into her new role with the same energy and level of commitment with which she had approached her fieldwork at Gombe. She believed it was almost a religious obligation. She began a furious campaign, traveling the world and lobbying lawmakers and

TACARE

TACARE is short for the Lake Tanganyika Catchment Reforestation and Education program. It's pronounced "take care," a phrase that neatly explains what the program is designed to do. The Jane Goodall Institute set up TACARE in 1994 to help people in villages near Gombe find ways to make money and live comfortably without endangering the natural environment. Education forms the core of the program, which teaches people better farming techniques and more healthful ways of eating and living. The ultimate purpose is to get local people involved in protecting and sustaining Gombe and its chimpanzees.

In later years, Goodall's conservation efforts extended to many species across the globe.

political leaders in Washington, DC, and other world capitals to make changes. Global warming, endangered species, inhumane treatment of animals in medical research, unrestricted economic growth, and deforestation were all problems Goodall believed governments and world leaders should work to fix. She saw it as her mission to keep pushing and prodding people to change their attitudes, pass new laws, and get involved in local efforts to save the planet before it was too late. "If we stop now, everything's going to go," she told a reporter. "So we have to keep on doing our best for as long as we can, and if we're going to die, let's die fighting."[6] By the 1990s, she was traveling

300 days every year, working and speaking tirelessly as what journalist Stephen Moss called "an environmental evangelist."[7]

When Goodall saw a film that had been made secretly inside Sema Inc., a medical research laboratory in Maryland, she was horrified. The film showed chimps in tiny cages, neglected and terrified, purposely infected with human diseases such as AIDS. The pictures were almost more than she could bear. She added the use of animals for medical research to her list of things to combat.

Goodall's highly publicized efforts during the next 20 years brought her into direct conflict with the powerful medical research industry. By extension, she received criticism from the medical industry itself—hospitals, doctors, nurses, and patients. Many saw her work as an attack on them and their equally heartfelt mission to help humanity. They said that in order to find cures for the multitude of diseases and conditions that plague humans, they had no choice but to use humankind's closest relatives to test new medicines and procedures.

Goodall conceded that "the use of animals in experiments is a highly controversial issue."[8] And yet, she still asked, "Regardless of how much or how little these experiments benefit human health, should we exploit animals in this way?"[9] She believed medical science must "find alternatives to the use of live animals of all species in experimentation."[10] But she understood it would take time for that level of change to happen. As a scientist, she realized immediately stopping all animal testing would not be in humanity's best interest.

Because of Goodall's repeated pleas, in the 1990s, Sema Inc. completely changed its chimp facility. It created comfortable and humane living spaces and retrained lab staff to interact better with the animals. In 2010, Goodall asked the head of the National Institutes of Health (NIH), the leading medical research agency in the United States, to eliminate or reduce the number of chimps used in US government research labs. Three years later, the NIH announced it would reduce its population of captive chimps from 350 to 50.[11] Goodall's urging also led thousands of people to write to the US Fish and Wildlife Service, asking it to raise the status of chimpanzees from threatened, or likely to become endangered, to endangered, or in danger of extinction. The Fish and Wildlife Service took that step in 2015.

"To me, cruelty is the worst of human sins. Once we accept that a living creature has feelings and suffers pain, then if we knowingly and deliberately inflict suffering on that creature we are equally guilty. Whether it be human or animal we brutalize *ourselves*."[12]

—*Jane Goodall*, Reason for Hope: A Spiritual Journey, *1999*

ROOTS & SHOOTS

In 1991, some young Tanzanian students asked Goodall how they could get involved in the work of animal and environmental conservation. That conversation led to the formation of the first Roots & Shoots group. Goodall designed the group to immerse young people in projects and activities to broaden their understanding of the natural world and empower them to find ways to preserve and protect it. She chose the name because, as she explained, "Roots creep quietly underground and make a new foundation; Shoots seem new and small—but to reach the light can move boulders."[13]

Roots & Shoots began with 12 students in Tanzania and has grown to 150,000 students in 130 countries.

Goodall was in New York City when terrorists attacked on September 11, 2001, an experience that gave her an even greater sense of urgency. In the days following the tragedy, she began to realize that the focus of Roots & Shoots and of her activism needed to turn more directly toward world peace and international understanding. She expressed these feelings in October 2001, when she received the Gandhi/King Award for Nonviolence, given by the World Movement for Nonviolence. Later, Goodall spoke of the enormous responsibility she felt attempting to live up to standards set by the two men the award honored, Mahatma Gandhi and Martin Luther King, Jr. She pointed to Roots & Shoots programs as a way to break down barriers and bridge religious and political divisions between nations. "We are truly sowing the seeds of global peace," she said.[14]

Still, Goodall felt she needed to do more. In a 2010 film called *Jane's Journey*, a weary-looking Goodall said, "I've been traveling around the world giving these messages, but clearly it's not enough. Clearly, I have to do more: inspire more people, gather more people, create a greater urgency."[15]

Goodall eventually came to believe that wild chimpanzee extinction is inevitable. As early as 1987, she said, "It seems not unlikely that the day will come when the only chimpanzees are in laboratories and zoos."[16] By 2003, only approximately 100 chimps still lived at Gombe.[17] By 2016, that number had fallen to 90.[18] A 2013 report published in the *Institute for Laboratory Animal Research Journal* said that even within protected areas, chimpanzees "are in danger of becoming extinct in our lifetimes."[19]

Even in the face of such dire circumstances, Goodall refused to give up. In 1999, she published *Reason for Hope: A Spiritual Journey*, which is essentially her religious autobiography. It presents reasons why, despite everything, she still has faith that humankind might somehow solve the enormous problems threatening its future existence. Her 2014 book *Seeds of Hope: Wisdom and Wonder from the World of Plants* is autobiographical as well. In it, Goodall challenges readers to consider the critical connection between plant life and human life on Earth.

Goodall continued to believe that one of the strongest reasons for hope is the energy and enthusiasm that can be found or kindled among young people. By 2016, more than 150,000 kids worldwide participated in the Roots & Shoots programs.[20]

Peace Doves

In April 2002, United Nations (UN) Secretary-General Kofi Annan named Goodall a UN Messenger of Peace in recognition of her commitment to the cause of world peace. As part of the ceremony, Goodall received a special pin in the shape of a dove, the traditional symbol of peace. Since that time, displaying dove puppets—giant flapping puppets made from recycled materials—has been part of Roots & Shoots events everywhere.

Even after half a century of research and activism, Goodall remains committed to doing more.

These students reflected Goodall's optimistic belief that the knowledge and enthusiasm of young people are the keys to saving the world. As she once said, "Nothing I've done to help people understand chimpanzees, and nothing we've done to protect them or the environment will matter if we don't raise a generation of children to be better stewards than we've been."[21]

TIMELINE

1934
On April 3, Jane Goodall is born in London, England.

1957
On March 13, Goodall boards a ship for Africa; Goodall begins working with Louis and Mary Leakey at Olduvai Gorge in Tanzania as a secretary and assistant.

1960
On July 14, Goodall and her mother, Vanne, travel to Gombe, where Goodall discovers chimps eating meat and using tools.

1961
After Goodall faces months of rejection and aggression by the chimps, David Graybeard accepts her, and the other chimps follow his lead.

1962
Goodall begins studying for her PhD at Cambridge University.

1963
Goodall's first article appears in *National Geographic* and is a popular, but not scientific, success.

1964
Goodall marries Hugo van Lawick.

1966
The chimps of Gombe are affected by a polio epidemic, and Goodall treats them with vaccines.

1967
Goodall publishes her first book, a children's book called *My Friends the Wild Chimpanzees*.

1968
Goodall publishes her doctoral dissertation, "Behaviour of Free-living Chimpanzees in the Gombe Stream Reserve" in the scientific journal *Animal Behaviour.*

1971
Goodall publishes her book *In the Shadow of Man* to much acclaim.

1974
Goodall observes a chimp civil war that results in the decimation of an entire population of chimps.

1975
Goodall marries Derek Bryceson, head of Tanzanian national parks; Goodall has to leave Gombe for her own safety after four student assistants are kidnapped.

1977
Goodall founds the Jane Goodall Institute.

1986
Goodall's book *The Chimpanzees of Gombe: Patterns of Behavior* is published to wide professional acclaim, and Goodall begins her work as an animal activist.

1991
Goodall organizes the Roots & Shoots program to involve young people in animal conservation.

2001
In October, Goodall receives the Gandhi/King Award for Nonviolence, given by the World Movement for Nonviolence.

ESSENTIAL
FACTS

DATE OF BIRTH
April 3, 1934

PLACE OF BIRTH
London, England

PARENTS
Mortimer and Vanne Morris-Goodall

EDUCATION
Cambridge University, PhD in ethology (1965)

MARRIAGES
Hugo van Lawick (married 1964, divorced 1974); Derek Bryceson (1975)

CHILDREN
Hugo Eric Louis (Grub) van Lawick

CAREER HIGHLIGHTS

- With the help of anthropologist Louis Leakey, Goodall founded the Gombe Stream Research Centre in 1965. She studied chimpanzee behavior there for nearly 25 years. At Gombe, Goodall discovered that chimpanzees made and used tools and hunted and ate meat. Her findings challenged long-held beliefs that only humans exhibited intelligence and emotions.

- In 1986, Goodall published *The Chimpanzees of Gombe: Patterns of Behavior*, the most complete collection of scientific data and information about chimpanzee behavior published to that point. Goodall wrote a number of other popular books about herself, her ideas, and her work, including *Reason for Hope* (1999) and *Seeds of Hope* (2014).

SOCIETAL CONTRIBUTIONS

- Goodall's methods and approaches to the study of animal behavior, seen as unscientific in 1960, are now considered standard in the field of ethology.
- Goodall influenced and inspired many scientists, particularly women, through her example and writing.
- Goodall founded the organization Roots & Shoots to encourage environmental conservation and world peace activities among young people worldwide.

CONFLICTS

- In the 1960s, Goodall faced prejudice against women entering the previously all-male field of ethology.
- Goodall struggled for acceptance of her research, for which she developed a new approach to ethology that involved watching and recording in the field.
- In her role as a vocal animal rights activist, Goodall faced criticism from scientists and the medical-research establishment for her opposition to the use of animals in medical research.

QUOTE

"Nothing I've done to help people understand chimpanzees, and nothing we've done to protect them or the environment will matter if we don't raise a generation of children to be better stewards than we've been." *–Jane Goodall*

GLOSSARY

alpha
A term used to describe the highest-ranking position in an animal group or society.

anthropologist
A scientist who studies the origin, behavior, and development of humans.

carnivorous
Meat-eating.

clinical
Scientifically detached and objective; the absence of emotion and feelings.

ethology
The study of animal behavior in the natural environment.

hominin
A member of a family of mammals that walk on two legs, including humans and human ancestors.

monograph
A scholarly piece of writing on a specific topic.

paleoanthropologist
A scientist who studies fossils of human ancestors.

primate
An order of mammals that live in complex social systems, exhibit intelligence, and have highly developed brains and opposable thumbs; examples include lemurs, monkeys, apes, and humans.

submission
The act of yielding or giving way to another.

ADDITIONAL RESOURCES

SELECTED BIBLIOGRAPHY

Goodall, Jane. *The Chimpanzees of Gombe: Patterns of Behavior.* Boston: Belknap, 1986. Print.

---. *In the Shadow of Man.* Boston: Houghton, 1971. Print.

---. *Reason for Hope: A Spiritual Journey.* New York: Warner, 1999. Print.

---. *Through a Window: My Thirty Years with the Chimpanzees of Gombe.* Boston: Houghton, 1990. Print.

Peterson, Dale. *Jane Goodall: The Woman Who Redefined Man.* Boston: Houghton, 2006. Print.

FURTHER READINGS

Allman, Toney. *Women Scientists and Inventors.* San Diego: ReferencePoint, 2017. Print.

Edwards, Roberta. *Who Is Jane Goodall?* New York: Grosset, 2012. Print.

Ottaviani, Jim. *Primates: The Fearless Science of Jane Goodall, Dian Fossey, and Biruté Galdikas.* New York: First Second, 2013. Print.

Silvey, Anita. *Untamed: The Wild Life of Jane Goodall.* Washington, DC: National Geographic, 2015. Print.

WEBSITES

To learn more about Women in Science, visit **abdobooklinks.com**. These links are routinely monitored and updated to provide the most current information available.

FOR MORE INFORMATION

For more information on this subject, contact or visit the following organizations:

The Jane Goodall Institute
1595 Spring Hill Road, Suite 550, Vienna, VA 22182
703-682-9220
http://www.janegoodall.org
The Jane Goodall Institute is the main organization supporting Jane Goodall's programs. Its initiatives include protecting great apes, ensuring healthy habitats, and using science and technology for conservation.

The Jane Goodall Institute's Chimpanzee Eden Sanctuary
47 R40, Barberton Road, Nelspruit, Mpumalanga, South Africa
+27 0 79 777 1514
http://www.chimpeden.com/
The Eden Sanctuary houses chimps that have been displaced from their natural habitats in Africa. Located in the Umhloti Nature Reserve, near Nelspruit, South Africa, the sanctuary is one of Jane Goodall's more cherished projects. Daily tours are available.

Lincoln Park Zoo
2001 North Clark Street, Chicago, IL 60614
312-742-2000
http://www.lpzoo.org/
Researchers at the Lincoln Park Zoo continue to study chimp behavior, tool use, and cognition. The zoo has partnered with Chimp Haven, a chimpanzee sanctuary, to improve the lives of chimps. The zoo also offers a free app aimed at allowing anyone to become an ethologist and chart the behavior of animals at any zoo or park, or even of pets at home.

Roots & Shoots
1595 Spring Hill Road, Suite 550, Vienna, VA 22182
703-682-9220
https://www.rootsandshoots.org
Supported by the Jane Goodall Institute, Roots & Shoots sponsors youth-led programs in communities around the world. Through the organization, young people work to address the needs of their community, animal welfare, and the environment.

SOURCE
NOTES

CHAPTER 1. CLOSE ENCOUNTERS

1. Jane Goodall. *The Chimpanzees of Gombe: Patterns of Behavior.* Cambridge, MA: Harvard UP, 1986. Print. 49.

2. Jane Goodall. *In the Shadow of Man.* Boston: Houghton, 1971. Print. 2.

3. Ibid. 19.

4. Dale Peterson. *Jane Goodall: The Woman Who Redefined Man.* Boston: Houghton, 2006. Print. 205.

5. Jane Goodall. *The Chimpanzees of Gombe: Patterns of Behavior.* Cambridge, MA: Harvard UP, 1986. Print. 270–271.

6. Ibid. 130.

7. Dale Peterson. *Jane Goodall: The Woman Who Redefined Man.* Boston: Houghton, 2006. Print. 212.

8. Carol Lee Flinders. *Enduring Lives: Portraits of Women and Faith in Action.* New York: Penguin, 2006. Print. 127.

9. Jane Goodall. *Africa in My Blood: An Autobiography in Letters: The Early Years.* Edited by Dale Peterson. Boston: Houghton, 2000. Print. 1–2.

CHAPTER 2. WILD BEGINNINGS

1. Dale Peterson. *Jane Goodall: The Woman Who Redefined Man.* Boston: Houghton, 2006. Print. 29.

2. Ibid. 18.

3. Ibid. 22.

4. Ibid. 11.

5. Sy Montgomery. *Walking with the Great Apes: Jane Goodall, Dian Fossey, Biruté Galdikas.* Boston: Houghton, 1991. Print. 201–202.

6. Jane Goodall. *Reason for Hope: A Spiritual Journey.* New York: Warner, 1999. Print. 20–21.

7. Carol Lee Flinders. *Enduring Lives: Portraits of Women and Faith in Action.* New York: Penguin, 2006. Print. 105.

8. Jane Goodall and Mark Bekoff. *The Ten Trusts: What We Must Do to Care for the Animals We Love.* San Francisco, CA: Harper, 2002. Print. 20.

9. Jane Goodall and Gail Hudson. *Seeds of Hope: Wisdom and Wonder from the World of Plants.* New York: Grand Central, 2014. Print. 57.

CHAPTER 3. AFRICA IN MY BLOOD

1. Dale Peterson. *Jane Goodall: The Woman Who Redefined Man.* Boston: Houghton, 2006. Print. 58.

2. Jane Goodall. *Africa in My Blood: An Autobiography in Letters: The Early Years.* Edited by Dale Peterson. Boston: Houghton, 2000. Print. 88.

3. Ibid. 82.

4. Ibid. 112.

5. Dale Peterson. *Jane Goodall: The Woman Who Redefined Man*. Boston: Houghton, 2006. Print. 117.

6. Londa Schiebinger. "Has Feminism Changed Science?" *Signs: Journal of Women and Culture in Society* 25.4 (Summer 2000): 1171–1175. Print.

7. Biruté Mary Galdikas. "The Vanishing Man of the Forest." *New York Times*. New York Times, 6 Jan. 2007. Web. 1 Oct. 2016.

8. Carol Lee Flinders. *Enduring Lives: Portraits of Women and Faith in Action*. New York: Penguin, 2006. Print. 114.

CHAPTER 4. GOMBE

1. Jane Goodall. *In the Shadow of Man*. Boston: Houghton, 1971. Print. 62.

2. Ibid. 49.

3. Ibid. 58.

4. Carol Lee Flinders. *Enduring Lives: Portraits of Women and Faith in Action*. New York: Penguin, 2006. Print. 122.

5. Dale Peterson. *Jane Goodall: The Woman Who Redefined Man*. Boston: Houghton, 2006. Print. 322.

6. Ibid. 324.

7. Sy Montgomery. *Walking with the Great Apes: Jane Goodall, Dian Fossey, Biruté Galdikas*. Boston: Houghton, 1991. Print. 127.

CHAPTER 5. BECOMING A SCIENTIST

1. Jane Goodall. "My Life among the Wild Chimpanzees." *National Geographic* 124.2 (August 1963): 274. Print.

2. Dale Peterson. *Jane Goodall: The Woman Who Redefined Man*. Boston: Houghton, 2006. Print. 336.

3. Ibid. 336.

4. Jane Goodall. *In the Shadow of Man*. Boston: Houghton, 1971. Print. 268.

5. Dale Peterson. *Jane Goodall: The Woman Who Redefined Man*. Boston: Houghton, 2006. Print. 294.

6. Jane Goodall. *Through a Window: My Thirty Years with the Chimpanzees of Gombe*. Boston: Houghton, 1990. Print. 16.

7. Sy Montgomery. *Walking with the Great Apes: Jane Goodall, Dian Fossey, Biruté Galdikas*. Boston: Houghton, 1991. Print. 128.

8. Ibid. 106.

9. Carol Lee Flinders. *Enduring Lives: Portraits of Women and Faith in Action*. New York: Penguin, 2006. Print. 138.

10. Jane Goodall. *Africa in My Blood: An Autobiography in Letters: The Early Years*. Edited by Dale Peterson. Boston: Houghton, 2000. Print. 186.

11. Sy Montgomery. *Walking with the Great Apes: Jane Goodall, Dian Fossey, Biruté Galdikas*. Boston: Houghton, 1991. Print. 116–117.

12. Dale Peterson. *Jane Goodall: The Woman Who Redefined Man*. Boston: Houghton, 2006. Print. 486.

13. Jane Goodall. *The Chimpanzees of Gombe: Patterns of Behavior*. Cambridge, MA: Harvard UP, 1986. Print. 503–504.

14. Ibid. 66.

15. Dale Peterson. *Jane Goodall: The Woman Who Redefined Man*. Boston: Houghton, 2006. Print. 325.

16. Sy Montgomery. *Walking with the Great Apes: Jane Goodall, Dian Fossey, Biruté Galdikas*. Boston: Houghton, 1991. Print. 39.

CHAPTER 6. DANGEROUS DAYS

1. Dale Peterson. *Jane Goodall: The Woman Who Redefined Man*. Boston: Houghton Mifflin, 2006. Print. 404.

2. Ibid. 409.

3. Peter Durantine. "Searching for the Cause of AIDS through Chimpanzee SIV." *Franklin & Marshall College*. Franklin & Marshall College, 16 Feb. 2016. Web. 10 Nov. 2016.

4. Jane Goodall. *Beyond Innocence: An Autobiography in Letters: The Later Years*. Edited by Dale Peterson. Boston: Houghton, 2001. Print. 122.

5. Dale Peterson. *Jane Goodall: The Woman Who Redefined Man*. Boston: Houghton, 2006. Print. 566.

6. Ibid. 465–466.

7. Jane Goodall. *In the Shadow of Man*. Boston: Houghton, 1971. Print. 129–130.

8. Jane Goodall. *Reason for Hope: A Spiritual Journey*. New York: Warner, 1999. Print. 117.

9. Jane Goodall. *The Chimpanzees of Gombe: Patterns of Behavior*. Cambridge, MA: Harvard UP, 1986. Print. 534.

10. Dale Peterson. *Jane Goodall: The Woman Who Redefined Man*. Boston: Houghton, 2006. Print. 481.

11. Ibid. 324.

12. Ibid.

13. Ibid. 481.

14. Ibid. 481–482.

15. Ibid. 491.

16. Jane Goodall. *Beyond Innocence: An Autobiography in Letters: The Later Years*. Edited by Dale Peterson. Boston: Houghton, 2001. Print. 145.

17. Dale Peterson. *Jane Goodall: The Woman Who Redefined Man*. Boston: Houghton, 2006. Print. 497.

CHAPTER 7. OMENS OF CHANGE

1. Dale Peterson. *Jane Goodall: The Woman Who Redefined Man*. Boston: Houghton, 2006. Print. 527.

2. Ibid.

3. Jane Goodall. *In the Shadow of Man*. Boston: Houghton, 1971. Print. 148.

4. Carol Lee Flinders. *Enduring Lives: Portraits of Women and Faith in Action*. New York: Penguin, 2006. Print. 124.

5. Robert S.O. Harding. "Geza Teleki (1943–2014)." *Primate Conservation*. BioOne, 2014. Web. 1 Oct. 2016.

6. Jane Goodall. *Reason for Hope: A Spiritual Journey*. New York: Warner, 1999. Print. 173.

7. Ibid. 174–175.

CHAPTER 8. NEW DIRECTIONS

1. Carol Lee Flinders. *Enduring Lives: Portraits of Women and Faith in Action*. New York: Penguin, 2006. Print. 158.

2. Cynthia Worsley, "Jane Goodall: Humanity and the Chimpanzee." *Journal of the Manitoba Anthropology Students' Association*. University of Manitoba, 2009. Web. 1 Oct. 2016.

3. Ibid.

4. Jane Goodall. *Reason for Hope: A Spiritual Journey*. New York: Warner, 1999. Print. 206.

5. Sy Montgomery. *Walking with the Great Apes: Jane Goodall, Dian Fossey, Biruté Galdikas*. Boston: Houghton, 1991. Print. 199.

6. Stephen Moss. "Jane Goodall: 'My Job Is to Give People Hope.'" *Guardian*. Guardian, 12 Jan. 2010. Web. 1 Oct. 2016.

7. Ibid.

8. Jane Goodall. *Reason for Hope: A Spiritual Journey*. New York: Warner, 1999. Print. 218.

9. Ibid. 219.

10. Ibid. 221.

11. Paul Tullis. "Jane Goodall Is Still Wild at Heart." *New York Times Magazine*. New York Times, 13 Mar. 2015. Web. 1 Oct. 2016.

12. Jane Goodall. *Reason for Hope: A Spiritual Journey*. New York: Warner, 1999. Print. 225.

13. Jane Goodall. *Beyond Innocence: An Autobiography in Letters: The Later Years*. Edited by Dale Peterson. Boston: Houghton, 2001. Print. 385.

14. Dale Peterson. *Jane Goodall: The Woman Who Redefined Man*. Boston: Houghton, 2006. Print. 659–660.

15. L. Knauer, director. *Jane's Journey*. First Run, 2010. Film.

16. Jane Goodall. *The Chimpanzees of Gombe: Patterns of Behavior*. Cambridge, MA: Harvard UP, 1986. Print. 593.

17. Paul Redfern. "Goodall: 'Trapped Gombe Chimps Face Extinction.'" *East African*. AllAfrica, 31 Mar. 2003. Web. 1 Oct. 2016.

18. Shawn Sweeney. Personal interview. 19 Nov. 2016.

19. Lori Gruen, Amy Fultz, and Jill Pruetz. "Ethical Issues in African Great Ape Field Studies." *ILAR Journal*. Oxford Academic. 1 Apr. 2013. Web. 1 Oct. 2016.

20. "About Us." *Jane Goodall's Roots and Shoots*. Jane Goodall Institute, n.d. Web. 17 Feb. 2017.

21. Carol Lee Flinders. *Enduring Lives: Portraits of Women and Faith in Action*. New York: Penguin, 2006. Print. 101.

INDEX

ABOUT THE
AUTHOR

Michael Capek is a former teacher and the author of numerous books for young readers. Beginning in the 1960s, he was inspired by *National Geographic* films and articles featuring Jane Goodall and her chimps. Like Goodall, he had a close relationship with a special animal in his childhood—his dog Lassie. Capek shares Goodall's love for animals and her support of youth conservation and peace programs locally and globally.